All About Skunks

Richard Tan

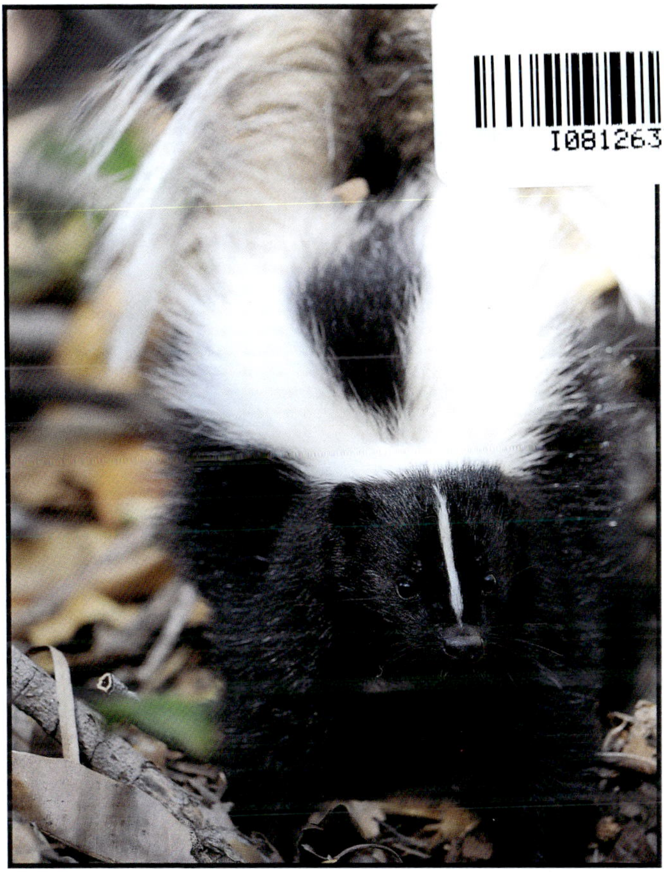

Rosen REAL READERS

Rosen Classroom™
New York

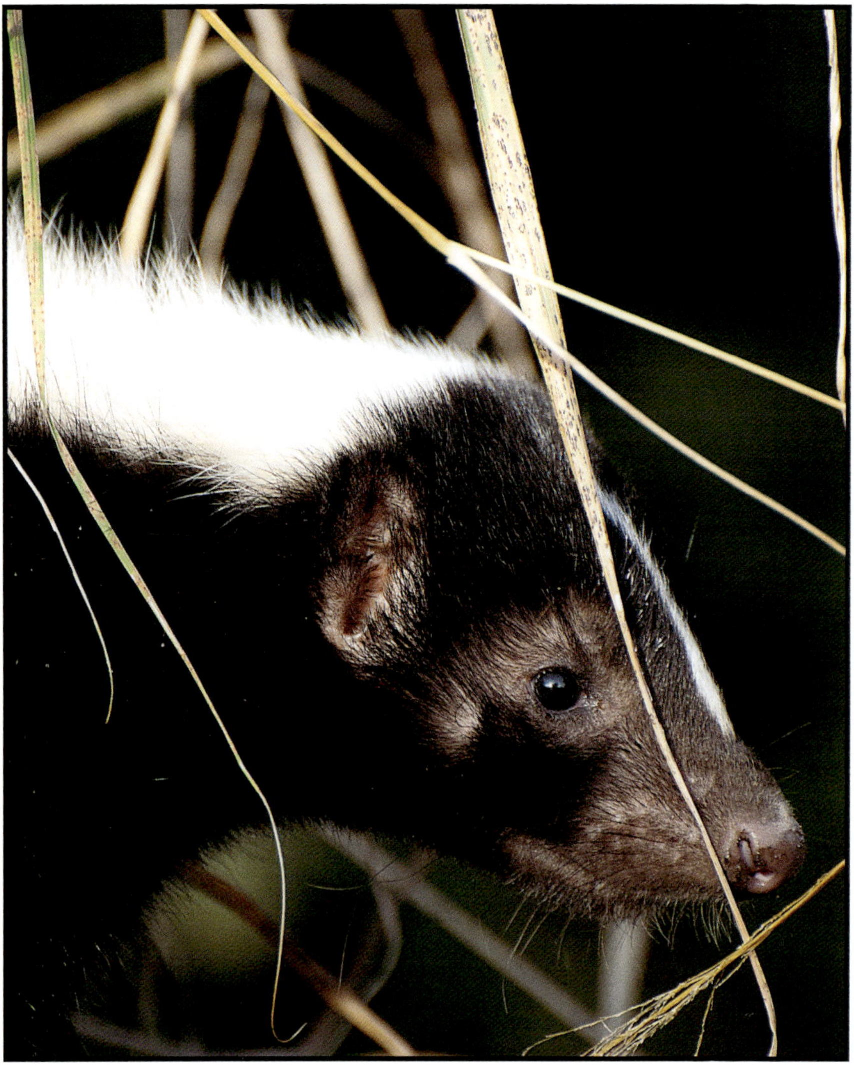

This is a skunk.

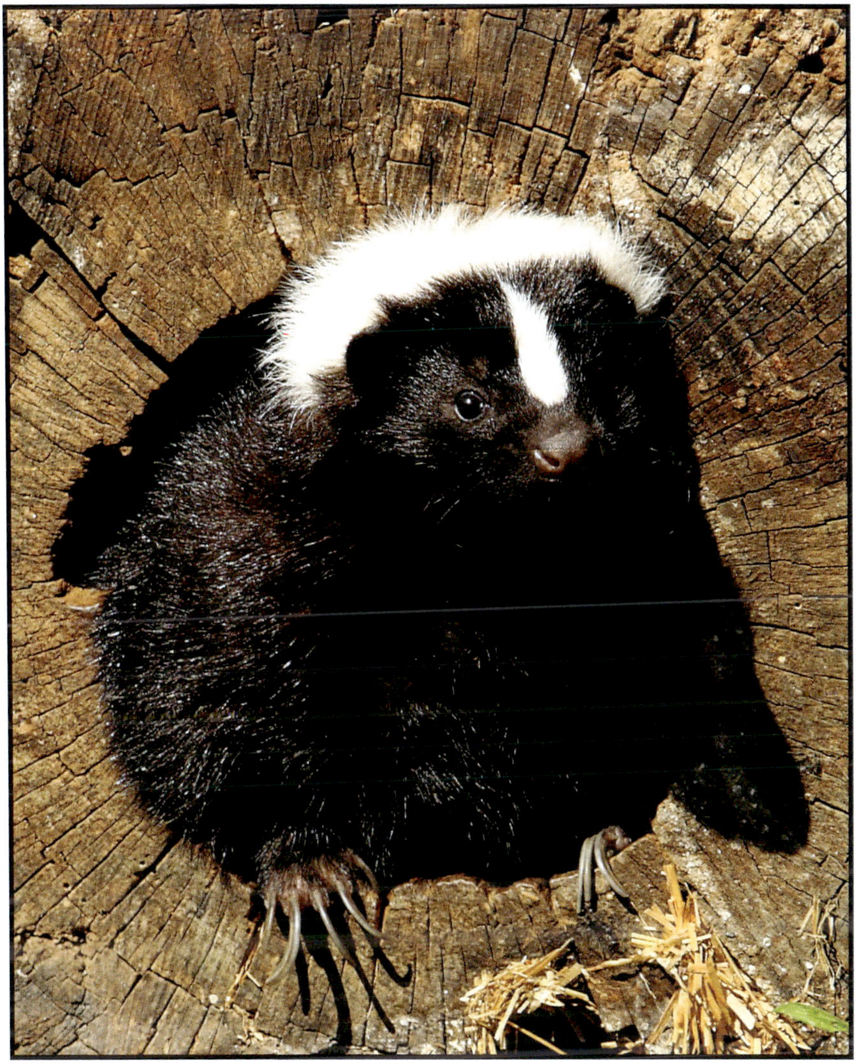

Skunks live in the woods.

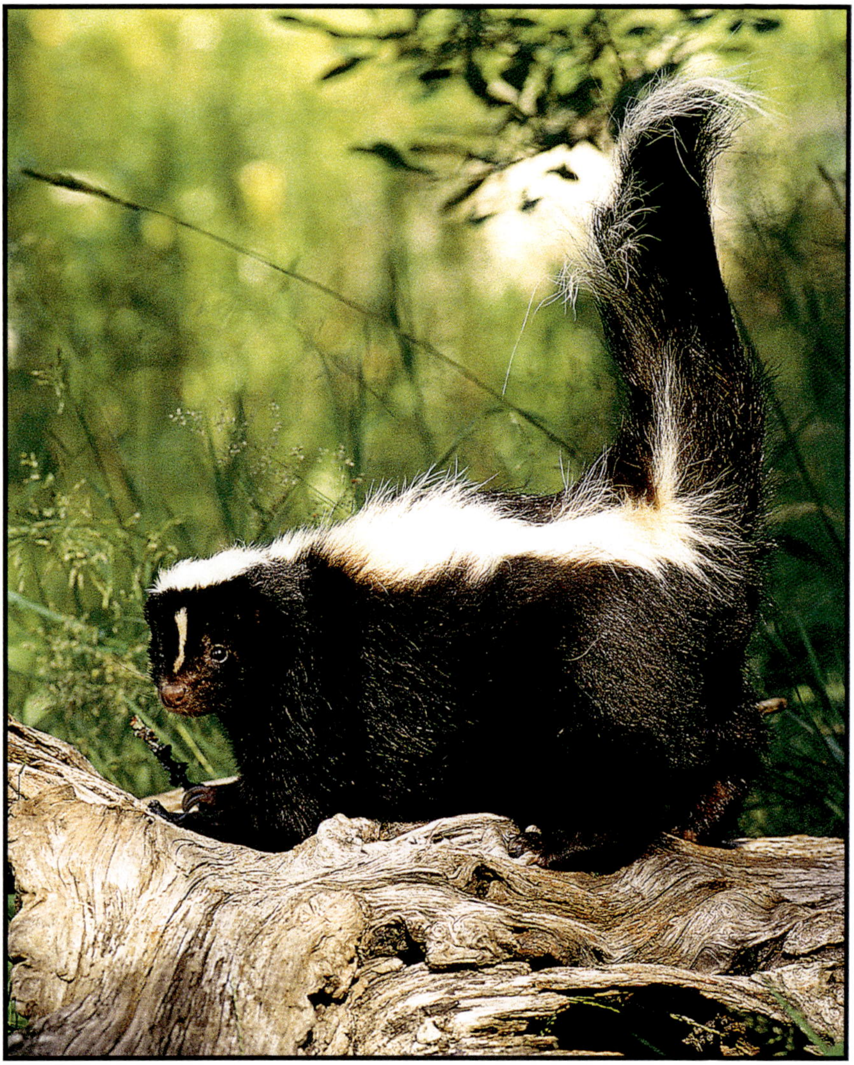

Skunks have stripes.

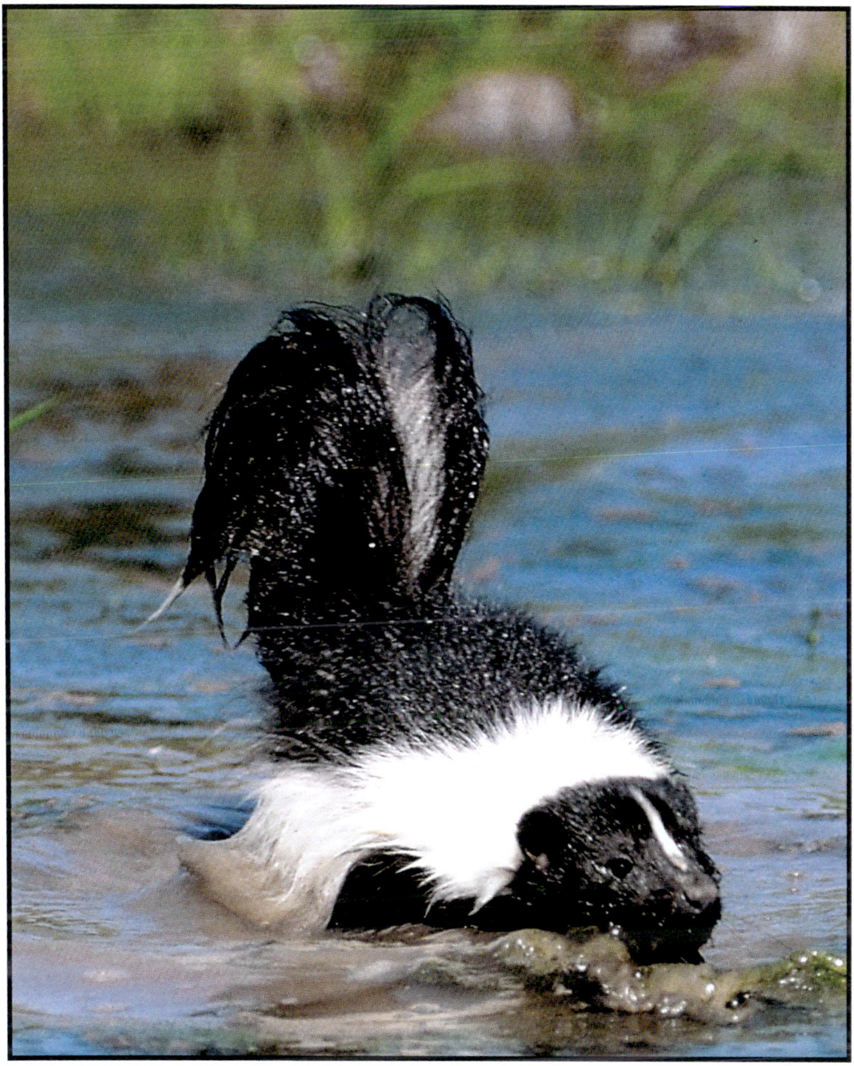

Skunks swim.

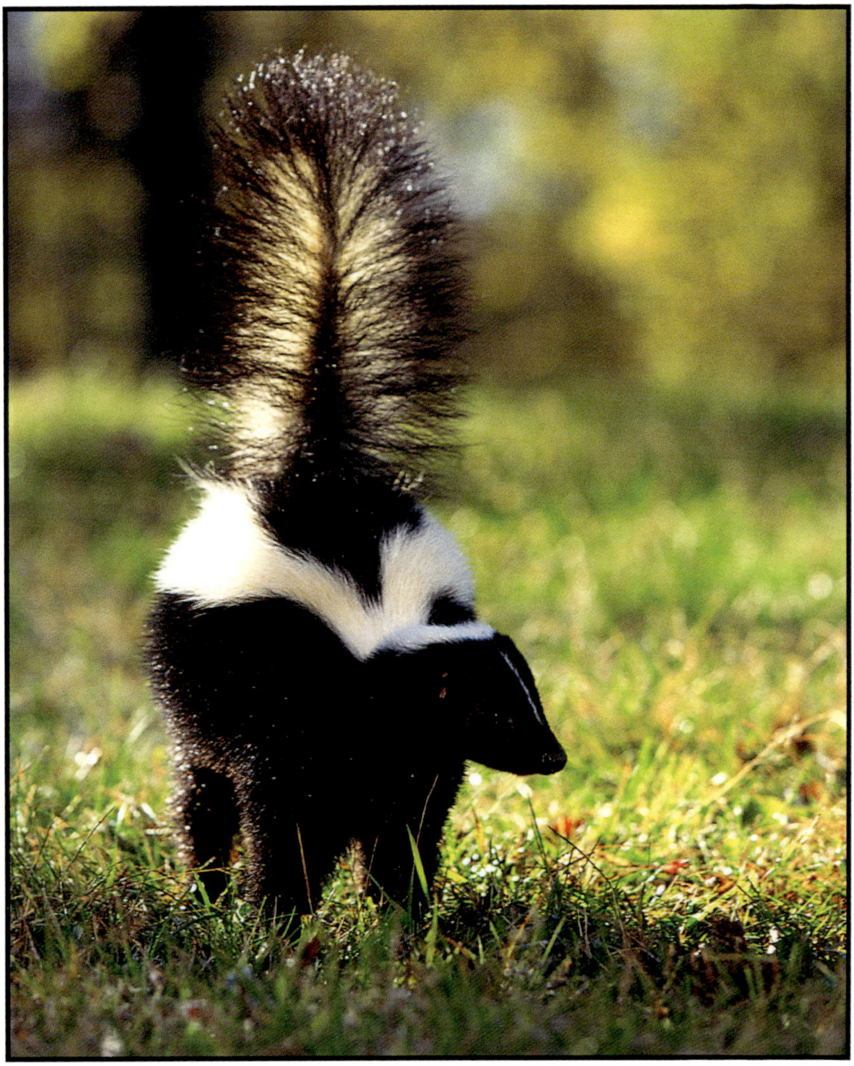

Skunks can smell bad.

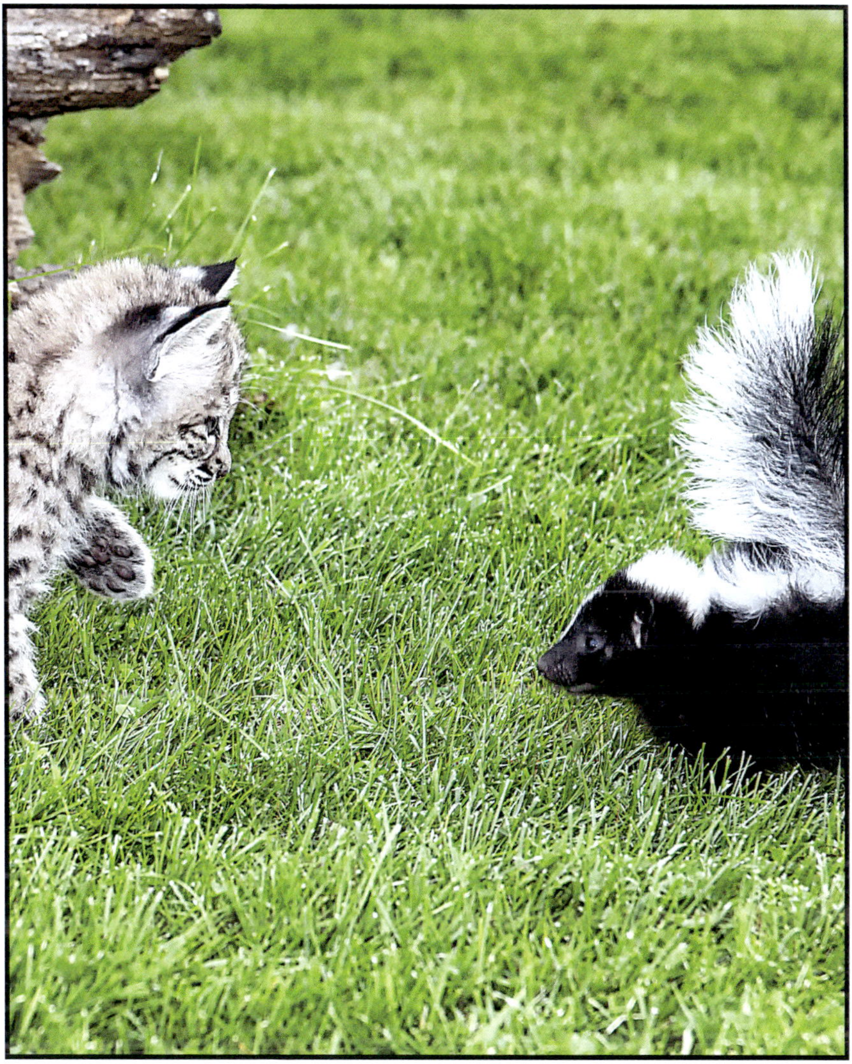

Skunks use smell to stay safe.

Words To Know

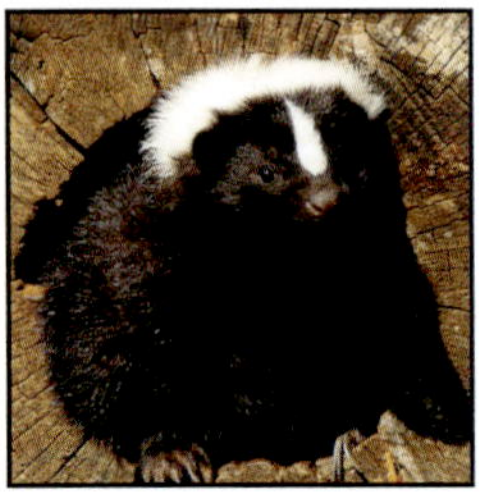

skunk

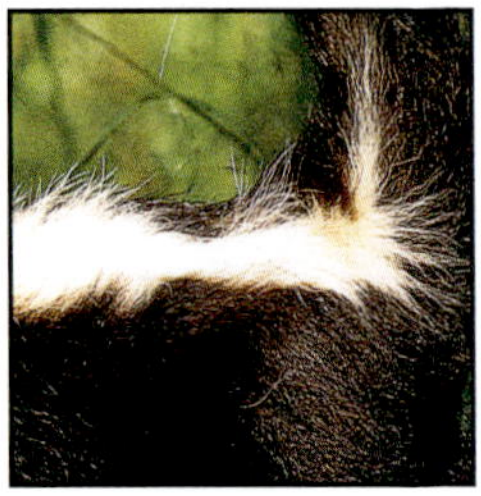

stripe

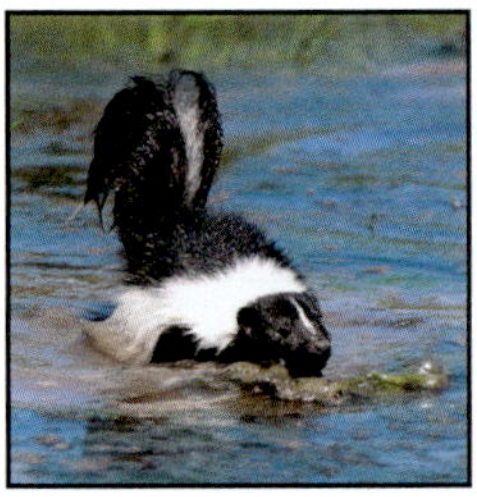

swim